SANCTUARY

A CANTATA OF HOPE AND PEACE

by Joseph M. Martin
Orchestrations by Stan Pethel

Performance Time: Approx. 40 minutes

(1) This symbol indicates a track number on the StudioTrax CD (Accompaniment Only) or SplitTrax CD.

ISBN 978-1-4950-0129-1

SHAWNEE 🕊 PRESS

Exclusively Distributed By

HAL•LEONARD®
CORPORATION

7777 W. BLUEMOUND RD. P.O. BOX 13819 MILWAUKEE, WI 53213

In Australia Contact:
Hal Leonard Australia Pty. Ltd.
4 Lentara Court
Cheltenham, Victoria, 3192 Australia
Email: ausadmin@halleonard.com.au

Visit Hal Leonard Online at
www.halleonard.com

Visit Shawnee Press Online at
www.shawneepress.com

FOREWORD

Throughout history, every culture has established sacred places of great religious significance. These places, great and small, are havens for seekers looking to discover a higher truth. They are preserved and set aside to encourage contemplation and meditation. They represent a gathering place for worship and a shelter for those in need. In these houses of faith, we encounter a holy hush that transcends the clamor of our daily enterprise. In their cloistered stillness, we sense the divine and learn to listen past our doubts and despair. Inspired, we fill these halls with our voices of adoration and decorate them with our songs of praise. When life brings tears, they are a retreat, a place to rest, where we remember God's promises of hope.

Beyond these houses of devotion, there is another sanctuary not made of brick or stone. This sacred haven is not decorated with colored glass or crowned with soaring steeples. This tabernacle of mercy comes to us with doors flung open wide like the arms of a loving parent. Into this cocoon of promise, we enter, unformed and vulnerable. We emerge transformed into a beautiful child of hope.

This living sanctuary is Jesus! Through Christ, God's tabernacle became flesh and moved among us. It is beneath this graceful shelter that we find our way through the wilderness and into our Promised Land. It is in Christ we find our fortress of faith, and there, wrapped in His everlasting love, we at last know the deep peace that surpasses our understanding. Our journey completed, the seeking over, we at last are home.

Joseph M. Martin

PERFORMANCE NOTES

SANCTUARY is a service in song that conveys the many ways in which the seeker finds shelter and safety in the grace of Christ. As the cantata shares moments in the Savior's life, we discover, by His example, the faithfulness of God's promises to His people. These important moments are supported in the work by narration, scripture, and song. Some directors may want to use simple images on banners or projections to further enhance the power of these concepts.

For the movement "Sanctuary of Grace," images of Old Testament covenants can be shown, such as the Ten Commandments, an ancient scroll, a rainbow, or a Lamb.

For "Shelter of Hope," the banner can reflect images of a boat in a storm, a cave entrance, or a child being embraced by a parent.

For "Hosanna! A Procession of Promise," images of a city fortress can be used or images of palm branches and a kingly crown.

For "In the Shadow of Your Wing," an image of a soaring eagle is best, or perhaps an image of the bread and cup.

For "Give to the Winds Your Fears," perhaps a sheltering tree, Jesus praying in the garden, or hands clasped in prayer.

For "Flee as a Bird," symbols associated with the cross would be best. The robe, the nails, and the crown of thorns are good possibilities.

For "Sanctuary of the Soul," symbols representing heaven, peace, and home would be most appropriate.

One ministerial extension of this cantata is to take an offering for the homeless or a local shelter for those in emotional and physical need. The message of this cantata is about celebrating the security we have in our faith, and remembering those who are vulnerable or disenfranchised allows the congregation to become a true song of hope in the lives of hurting people. This intersection of artistry and ministry may be the most important part of presenting this musical service of worship.

Much grace…

Joseph M. Martin

PRELUDE OF PEACE

Tune: *FINLANDIA*
by JEAN SIBELIUS (1865-1957)
Arranged by
JOSEPH M. MARTIN (BMI)

SANCTUARY - SATB

NARRATOR:

I will make a covenant of peace with them, an everlasting covenant. I will bless them...increase their numbers, and establish My sanctuary among them forever. *(Ezekiel 37:26, paraphrased)*

SANCTUARY OF GRACE

Words and music by
JOSEPH M. MARTIN (BMI)

With tender sincerity (♩ = ca. 66-68)

ACCOMP.

SOPRANO / ALTO *(opt. solo)*

There is a room, a qui - et place, an in - ner cham-ber made of grace; a place of peace and child - like

8

God, rest in the lov-ing arms of God.

(end solo)

(end solo)

mp

③

SOPRANO

ALTO

There is a room, a-dorned in

TENOR

BASS

mp

mp

light, a shrine of truth, a chap - el bright; a place to

pray, to seek, to find, a sa-cred space_____ of love di-

vine. There is a ref - uge from the cold, a heal-ing

ha - ven for the soul, a dwell-ing filled with gen - tle

lov - ing arms of God, rest in the lov-ing arms of God.

There is a tow - er stand-ing

tall, a soar-ing sym-bol o - ver all, and those who

gath-er to___ this place will find re - demp - tion, love and

grace. Come to the home near God's own heart, where hope be -

gins and heal - ing starts. Come to the cross, the rift - ed

* Tune: FINLANDIA, Jean Sibelius, 1865-1957
Words: "Be Still, My Soul" by Katharina von Schlegel, b. 1697; tr. Jane Borthwick, 1813-1897

NARRATION:

Hear now the word of Scripture.

For God so loved the world that He gave His one and only Son, that whoever believes in Him shall not perish but have eternal life.
(John 3:16 NIV*)

This promise declares a sanctuary of grace over the people of God. It is in this fortress of faith we find the eternal security that brings a peace that passes all understanding. The prophet Samuel declared his confidence in the living God, proclaiming:

"The Lord is my rock, my fortress and my deliverer; God is my rock, and my refuge. God is my shield and the horn of my salvation. He is my stronghold, my refuge and my Savior. From the evil of violence You save me." *(2 Samuel 22:2-3, NIV* paraphrased)*

In Jesus of Nazareth, this scripture became available to all people. Jesus became the Rock in a weary land. His ministry brought hope to the weary, and healing to the wounded. He became the sanctuary for the wanderer and a home for the wayfarer. Jesus became the sinner's hiding place and a shelter in the time of storm.

SHELTER OF HOPE

Words:
Traditional Spirituals

Tunes: **WEARY LAND**
WAYFARING STRANGER
Traditional Spirituals
Arranged by
JOSEPH M. MARTIN (BMI)

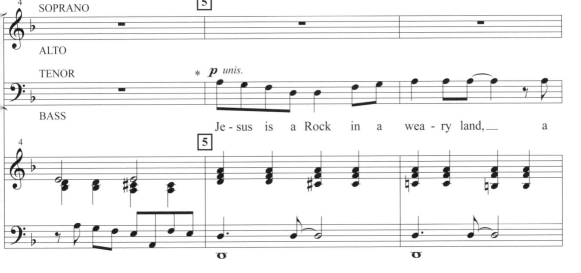

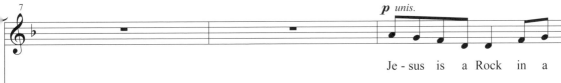

* Tune: WEARY LAND, traditional Spiritual
Words: "A Shelter in the Time of Storm" by Ira D. Sankey

* Tune: WAYFARING STRANGER, traditional Spiritual
Words: traditional Spiritual

SANCTUARY - SATB

woe; and when I walk_____ the path of

world of woe. *Oo*_____

sor - rows,____ I know I nev - er walk a-

I know I nev - er walk a-

lone. The road is long,_____ my load is heav - y. I trav-eled

lone.

NARRATION:

Jesus went from village to village preaching the good news of the Kingdom of God. Eventually, His journeys brought Him to a hill above the great city of Jerusalem. Looking over the holy city, He was moved to tears.

"Jerusalem, Jerusalem, you who kill the prophets and stone those God sends to you, how often I have longed to gather your children together, as a hen gathers her chicks under her wings, and you were not willing." *(Matt. 23:37, NIV* paraphrased)*

Soon, Jesus would enter the city and the people would gather to praise Him as their deliverer. A parade of worshippers waving palms and crying, "Hosanna, blessed is the One who comes in the name of the Lord," followed Him through the city. For a moment, it appeared that all the people were gathering within the shelter of God's loving wings of mercy.

HOSANNA! A PROCESSION OF PROMISE

Words and music by
JOSEPH M. MARTIN (BMI)

Lift up your heads, ye__ might-y gates, ye

SANCTUARY - SATB

ev - er - last - ing doors. To Zi - on comes the
cho - sen Son, the glo - ry of the Lord. Fling
o - pen wide the cit - y gates! Re - demp - tion draw - eth

nigh. Let ev - 'ry voice, in__ praise, re - joice, and

sing un - to the Lord, most high.

Great

Great Da - vid's Son, the__

34

SANCTUARY - SATB

NARRATION:

When it became time for Jesus and His chosen disciples to celebrate the Passover, they sought the quiet cloister of an upper room where a meal had been prepared. As they sat at the table, Jesus comforted them and announced to them a new covenant. This covenant of grace would be a sanctuary for all people. As the children of Israel took shelter from death and pestilence in the days of Moses, so would the Lamb of God provide a safe haven against spiritual death. Jesus would become God's sacrifice for the sins of all. For it is written, "Behold the Lamb of God, who takes away the sins of the world." *(John 1:29, NIV* paraphrased)*

lovingly dedicated to Eleanor J. Racek,
in celebration of forty-seven years of devoted service and direction in music ministry;
commissioned by the Chancel Choir, St. Charles Borromeo Catholic Church, Tacoma, Washington

IN THE SHADOW OF YOUR WING

Words by
JOSEPH M. MARTIN (BMI)

Music by
JOSEPH M. MARTIN
and DAVID ANGERMAN (ASCAP)

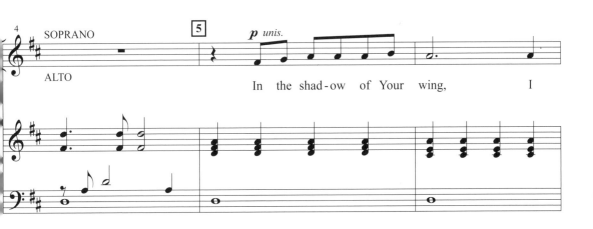

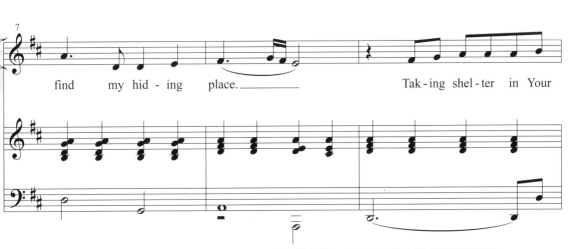

SANCTUARY - SATB

love,   I   rest   up - on   Your   per - fect   grace! ____

In Your chap-el made of   hope,   I   lift   my qui - et

praise, _____   for   in   the   shad - ow   of   Your

42

prayer, _____ for in the shad - ow of Your
wing, I ____ know _____ Your ten - der
care.

* Words: Charles Wesley, 1707-1788

SANCTUARY - SATB

heart, I find in You my prom - ised life. ____

In Your chap - el made of joy, I

sing un - to my Lord. ____ For in the shad - ow

48

NARRATION:

After the Passover meal, Jesus took sanctuary in a garden on the Mount of Olives, called Gethsemane. He had often come to this place to pray, and, as He knelt beneath a canopy of trees, He felt deep anguish in His spirit. As deep shadows began to fall, three times He prayed to His Father, "Let this cup pass by Me." And three times He cried, "Thy will be done." His heart was in despair, so God sent an angel who comforted and ministered to Him.

By His example, Jesus in the garden taught us to take refuge in the sanctuary of prayer. It is in that chapel of hope and light that we are able to find peace in the midst of life's challenges. It is in these quiet moments of reflection that we may feel the winds of God's Spirit moving in our midnight gardens, refreshing us with perfect grace.

in memory of Coger Robertson of Central Baptist Church, Bearden, Knoxville, TN (1997-2012)

GIVE TO THE WINDS YOUR FEARS

Words by
PAUL GERHARDT (1607-1676)
Translation by
JOHN WESLEY (1703-1791), alt.

Music by
JOSEPH M. MARTIN (BMI)

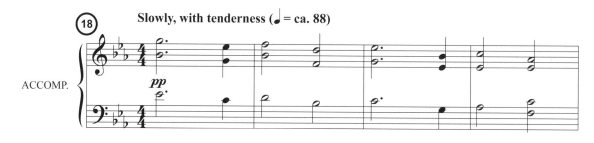

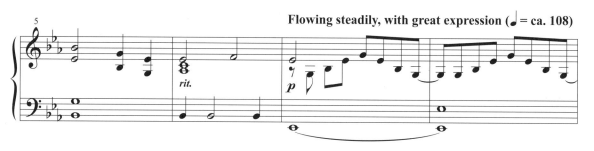

SANCTUARY - SATB

52

in His hands;_____ to

His sure truth and ten - der_____

care,_____ who earth and heav'n com -

winds your___ fears, your fears.___

fears.___

In hope be un - dis - mayed.___

God hears your sighs,___ and

62

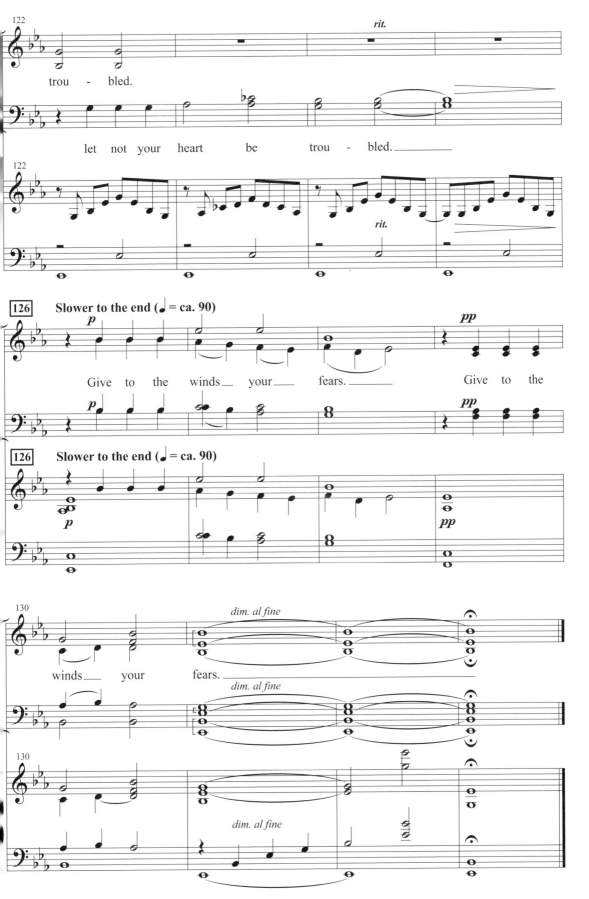

NARRATION:

Jesus was arrested and tried for treason before a Roman governor. Encouraged by an angry mob, Pilate ordered that Christ be beaten, and then delivered over to be executed by crucifixion. He was taken to a mountaintop where He was hung on a cross. This fulfilled the scripture that promised, "If I be lifted up, I will draw people everywhere to My side." *(John 12:32, paraphrased)*

As the skies darkened, Jesus whispered, "It is finished," and took upon His wounded heart the sins of the world.

His cross has become a hiding place for a desperate world. It is a tower of strength to the weak and a sanctuary of grace for the lost. In the sheltering embrace of His perfect love, the seeker at last finds home.

FLEE AS A BIRD

Words by
MARY S. B. DANA (1810-1883), alt.

Tune: **FLEE AS A BIRD**
by MARY S. B. DANA
Arranged by
JOSEPH M. MARTIN (BMI)

ACCOMP.

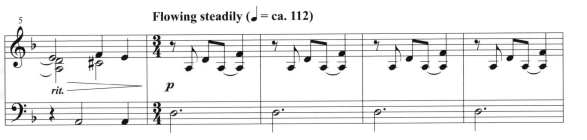

SOPRANO / ALTO

Flee as a bird to the moun - tain,

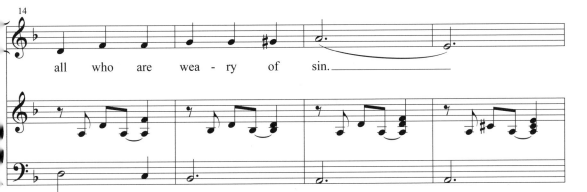

all who are wea - ry of sin.

SANCTUARY - SATB

66

Christ, in His arms, will bear you,

all who are wea-ry from sin.

rit. *a tempo* (end solo)

SOPRANO
ALTO
Oo
TENOR
BASS
He is the boun-ti-ful Giv - er.

68

Come, for the Lord is near you.

Call, and the Sav - ior will hear you.

Christ, in His arms, will bear you,

all who are wea-ry of sin, oh,

all who are wea-ry of sin.

78 With sweeping emotion (♩ = ca. 108)

78 With sweeping emotion (♩ = ca. 108)

shel- tered so ten- der - ly there.

Call, for the Lord is near you.

Call, for the Sav - ior will hear you.

Christ, in His arms, will bear you,

all who are wea-ry of sin, oh,

all who are wea-ry of sin.

NARRATION:

Jesus is the Ark of Safety.

Jesus is my Rock, a Mighty Fortress, my Deliverer.

Jesus is a Tower of Strength.

Jesus is my Refuge and Strength, a very present help in the time of trouble.

God is my Shield, my Glory. He lifts up my head.

Jesus is the Ark of Promise against the tempests of life.

Jesus is my Hiding Place. The Lord preserves me from trouble.

The Lord is the Shade at my right hand.

Jesus is my Dwelling Place, and underneath are the everlasting arms.

Jesus is my Keeper, and in His loving grace, I find my sanctuary.

SANCTUARY OF THE SOUL

Incorporating
"Beneath the Cross of Jesus"
"It Is Well with My Soul"
and "Be Still, My Soul"
Arranged by
JOSEPH M. MARTIN (BMI)

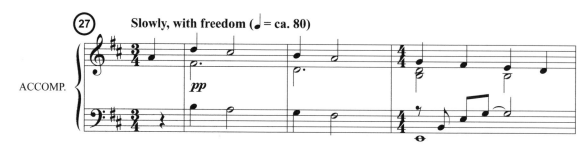

* Tune: ST. CHRISTOPHER, Frederick C. Maker, 1844-1927
Words: Elizabeth C. Clephane, 1830-1869

SANCTUARY - SATB

fain would take my stand; the shad - ow of a

might - y rock, with - in a wea - ry land,

a home with - in the wil - der - ness, a

78

rest up-on the way, from the burn - ing of the
noon - tide heat, and the bur - den of the day.

SANCTUARY - SATB

* Tune: VILLE DU HAVRE, Philip P. Bliss, 1838-1876
   Words: Horatio G. Spafford, 1828-1888
** Tune: FINLANDIA, Jean Sibelius, 1865-1957
   Words: Katharina von Schlegel, b.1697; tr. Jane Borthwick, 1813-1897
† If tenors sing the cued notes, sopranos and altos should sing their top two notes.   SANCTUARY - SATB

ly the cross of grief and pain.

when

Leave to your sor - rows like sea bil - lows roll.

God to or - der and pro - vide._____

In ev - 'ry change, God faith - ful will re -

main. What ev - er my

lot,____ Thou hast taught____ me to say, "It is____

82

well. It is well with my

soul." Be still, my soul. Your

Lord, your lov - ing Friend_____ through thorn - y

POSTLUDE OF PEACE

Tune: **FINLANDIA**
by JEAN SIBELIUS (1865-1957)
Arranged by
JOSEPH M. MARTIN (BMI)

SANCTUARY - SATB